From Psychic to Soul

By

Diane Lewis

For permission, serialization, condensation, adaptions, or for our catalog of other publications, write to Ozark Mountain Publishing, Inc., P.O. Box 754, Huntsville, AR 72740, ATTN: Permissions Department.

Library of Congress Cataloging-in-Publication Data

Lewis, Diane – 1960 -
From Psychic to Soul by Diane Lewis

This book is a reveal of how every person is psychic, how we already, knowingly or not, use our abilities and how we can expand on them with easy-to-understand real-life examples. It further introduces little-known concepts as well as concepts I have created for understanding. You will also learn what your soul is and the concepts surrounding it.

1. Psychic 2. Soul 3. Paranormal 4. Metaphysical
I. Diane Lewis, 1960- II. Psychic III. Metaphysical IV. Soul V. Title

Library of Congress Catalog Card Number: 2017953718
ISBN: 9781940265452

Cover Art and Layout: www.vril8.com
Book set in: Times New Roman, Papyrus
Book Design: Tab Pillar
Published by:

PO Box 754, Huntsville, AR 72740
800-935-0045 or 479-738-2348; fax 479-738-2448
WWW.OZARKMT.COM

Printed in the United States of America

To Ma & Dad,
I miss our chats at the kitchen table

Contents

Contents

Introduction

Do you know there's more to this physical universe than meets the eye? Psychic ability is not for a chosen few but for those willing to expand and move beyond the confines of their world. It's not for the faint of heart or for those unwilling to stretch their imaginations to see what's possible. It's for all of you who feel the calling deep in your being and struggle for understanding.

From Psychic to Soul is a reveal of how every person is psychic, how we already, knowingly or not, use our abilities and how we can expand on them with easy-to-understand real-life examples. It further introduces little-known concepts as well as concepts I have created for understanding. You will also learn what your soul is and the concepts surrounding it.

As a psychic medium I discovered my abilities at a young age, and as they matured I sought to better understand these psychic experiences in order to further develop and refine my gift. Over the last twenty-five years, besides having firsthand knowledge of psychic, paranormal, and supernatural occurrences, my true talent lies in the ability to help people just like you connect with the spiritual realm and lead you to uncover your own greatness.

So allow me to take you on a journey, where you'll be enlightened about the mysteries that surround not only your psychic ability but also your soul.

PSYCHIC

Your Psychic Abilities

Do you know you're psychic? Everyone is, naturally.

You connect with and use your psychic abilities all the time because being psychic is actually your birthright.

Where It Started

This didn't just begin, you being psychic. This has always been, for everyone. Through the ages there have been people who were noted as psychic because they fully utilized their abilities. These individuals have been referred to as fortune tellers, seers, prophets, clairvoyants, mystics, and, yes, psychics.

Throughout history there are countless references. Psychics were called on to give guidance and insight.

Battle leaders found it vital to know the best time to go into combat. Court intrigue necessitated one to have insight for survival. And even farmers wanted predictions for how their crops would fair.

From royalty to presidents and everyday people, psychic ability, although today not totally accepted, has played a role throughout history.

So What Is a Psychic?

So exactly what is a psychic? Well, a psychic is a person who has the ability to read energy. The definition is someone who is sensitive to influences or forces of a nonphysical nature. In the scientific community they refer to psychic abilities as ESP, which stands for extrasensory perception—a perception that's occurring beyond our normal senses. Some simply refer to it as the sixth sense.

History

But somewhere along the timeline, your psychic abilities went from being a part of who you are to something considered outside of yourself. It became some rare talent that only a few people possessed, instead of a wonderful part of who you are. It became a shadow no one should see.

When we gaze through history we discover individuals who understood what we are capable of. They were steadfast in their resolve to enlighten us. A few even became great spiritual leaders. Dating all the way back to Abraham we have consistently seen those who understood our potential, but sadly over the centuries the true translation seems to have been lost to many.

To put more distance between our abilities, the Middle Ages brought with it fear. The psychic element, because of political and religious power, was changing. Many were smart to keep their abilities hidden, as revealing it could be a matter of life or death.

For instance, in 1431 Joan of Arc was burned at the stake for heresy. Her psychic abilities (her visions and voices), which had helped her win battles, were turned against her. At that period in time a woman in power, especially one who led in battles, was definitely a threat. So when she was captured, the king she served failed to help her.

Best known for his book *The Prophecies*, which was published in 1555, Nostradamus chose to write his prophecies in quatrains because he understood that in his day being beheaded was a real possibility if he posed a threat with his abilities.

The supernatural took an ugly turn in the late 1600s with the Salem witch trials where women were sentenced to death by hanging as a result. But in today's research of that event it is believed that the supernatural may have played a small role in the overall reasons for the hangings. Fear, dynamics, and possibility of a fungus may have also been contributing factors.

But by the 1840s the spiritualist movement emerged and continues to this day, and early in the 1900s emerged "the sleeping prophet" Edgar Cayce. Cayce, while in an unconscious state, conducted psychic readings ranging from diagnosing illnesses to revealing past lives and also future prophecies. The ARE (The Association for Research and Enlightenment), which was founded by Cayce, is still in existence today.

But even with so much publicity over the last century or so, psychic ability seemed destined for the background.

However, a quiet interest in the psychic phenomena in 1978 was undertaken by the U.S. government. The U.S. Army established the Stargate Project to investigate the potential for psychic development that could be used for military application.

This all stemmed from a belief that the Soviets during the cold war were funding research in this area.

Nevertheless in 1995 (just twenty-two years ago) the project was terminated by the CIA. There are reports that the CIA had used remote viewers, psychic spies if you will, for intelligence gathering.

Today, an emergence for understanding and using psychic abilities is reappearing and not just to government or to special individuals. Everyday people are starting to feel their birthright and are searching, just like you.

Unfortunately, we have been conditioned that the whole persona of psychic is either something other than what we really are or something to be hidden. Remember, people were persecuted for speaking out.

In today's world, the paranormal, the category where psychic falls, tends to conjure up all sorts of fearful and even evil images.

I'm going to unveil the misconceptions surrounding psychic abilities and bring it into the light where it truly belongs.

Your Universe

To begin with, to learn about your abilities requires a basic understanding of your universe.

Your natural world is one made up of energy and vibration. Spiritual, supernatural, and paranormal phenomenon is all connected to this source. Therefore, when referencing what is surrounding an event or occurrence these words, energy and vibration, are commonly used interchangeably.

So let's begin our journey by breaking down our world.

First of all, we have to address what **we** are. If we take away the physical aspect of ourselves, what's left? Our energy. We are nothing but energy. In our true form we are eternal energy beings.

So when we enter this physical world it's our energy that enters and infuses into all the cells of a form that's waiting exclusively for us.

But just because we're infusing in matter doesn't change the fact that at our core we are energy beings. Even our physical bodies are really energy. You see, quantum physicists discovered that physical atoms are made up of energy that is constantly spinning and vibrating. And our bodies are a collection of 7 billion, billion, billion atoms put together. That's 7 followed by 27 zeros.

So based on that reality and the additional fact that everything in our world is made up of billions upon billions of atoms, our world simply is an energy-based one.

What Makes You Psychic?

Then how does this make you psychic? Well, if everything is energy and you read energy, which you all have at some point or another, then it's common, you're psychic.

Let's take a look at animals.

Oodles of people believe their pets are psychic, and perhaps you're one of them. Any proud animal lover will tell you, myself included, that they communicate with their pets and their companions communicate back without the use of a common language to connect us. So how does this amazing feat happen? By reading energy. Our buddies sense our moods by reading our energy. If we're a bit out of sorts, we can count on our little pals to try to cheer us up.

It's the same for us. When we notice our favorite friend not being themselves we tend to just know what's wrong or at the very least that something is wrong. You are more than reading their body language; you are also reading their energy.

In addition to animals, birds and even insects (can you believe it?!) are great at reading the natural energy of our planet. They tend to know ahead of time when a natural disaster is going to strike from the energy or vibrations being emitted. Animals, birds, and insects read electromagnetic energy, vibrations, or soundwaves, and people can also read them.

Once I was working alone in my office when around 2:00 in the afternoon I suddenly began to feel really weird. The energy had changed around me causing me to feel disoriented, tired, and just not myself. I knew something was affecting me although I couldn't figure out what. After about five minutes it was so intense, I had to go lie down and ride it out.

About a half an hour later the feeling totally disappeared. I felt back to normal but wondered what had happened. What was it? I had no way of knowing at that point. It wasn't until later when I flipped on the five o'clock news that I discovered that a slight earthquake had gone through the area at the same time I felt the strange energy.

So now let's begin our exploration of our psychic abilities. When we're babies we read energy all the time. We feel energy and vibrations all around us. It just is, naturally.

Starting in infancy, babies respond to the energy around them. If the energy is calm, then the baby may tend to drift off to sleep without any fanfare. But if the energy is chaotic and charged then most likely the baby will respond in kind.

As children grow and develop, some will sense more than others the unseen forces around them. They may even have experiences and display talents that will follow them into adolescence and then adulthood. For other kids, whatever talents they may have begun to display sometimes seem to mysteriously disappear.

Your psychic ability actually has not disappeared. It's still there. It could however have become suppressed or shut down and that can happen for any number of reasons. For instance, if children have a frightening experience, that could shut things down really fast. Or they could have turned off their psychic antenna because of a whole host of reasons ranging all the way from family and peer acceptance, fears themselves in the supernatural, or religious upbringing or beliefs. These factors can and often do retard psychic development.

Interestingly, I have found that any given number of people will believe kids can be psychic but then they forget that those kids grow up and become adults.

Reading Energy

So how do we read energy? How is it actually done? Through this marvelous creation called our body. We use this physical mass.

You see, our bodies are like one giant nuclear reactor. Think about all those atoms. All 7 billion, billion, billion of them. All vibrating. All pumping out energy. All the time.

In addition to that, we have different systems in our bodies that work with energy. But here's the amazing part: like atoms, you can't see any of these other systems.

Mind

The first energy system is your mind. We're not talking about your brain, that's an organ; we're talking about your mind. So what is it? Your mind is the world of thoughts, feelings, attitudes, beliefs, and imagination. It's where you think your thoughts. And what are your thoughts? They are energy. Every thought you think is energy. It's a vibration that's emitted, similar to a radiowave.

Let us take a moment and think about our thoughts as energy. If you're sad in your mind, you think sad, you feel sad, and you project a sad vibration. The people around you will feel your sadness to some degree. If you're happy in your mind and you think happy, you feel happy and you project a happy vibration. The people will feel your happiness as well. Your energy emits a vibration outward that others can read.

Your thinking can bring about changes since you put energy behind your thoughts. You can take something you're thinking about and bring it into creation. We do it every day.

Your mind is powerful energy. With your mind you have the capability to be the master of your universe. You have the power to create it any way you choose, externally as well as internally.

Chakras

Another energy system we have is a series of orbs called chakras. Just a note, they have nothing to do with ghosts. These orbs start at the base of our trunk and end at our crown. The chakras follow our spine, giving coverage to our entire trunk.

The earliest writings about chakras stem from ancient writings and date back to the beginning of Eastern Indian culture. Each chakra connects with different aspects of your being and with your organs and feelings.

Have you ever experienced a gut feeling at one time or another? Your solar plexus or your gut is the most open area for psychic impressions on your body, and it just so happens to be a chakra center.

Meridians

And that's not all! Inside, covering what the chakras seem to miss, are meridians. Meridians are similar to our nerve network in that they run throughout our bodies. The Chinese call the energy that flows through the meridians qi (chi). They are the first known to utilize the meridian system around 100 BC for acupuncture.

Qi (chi) runs throughout our bodies, but the belief is that if the energy doesn't flow correctly or is blocked then illness and problems with the physical body can result. You see, qi (chi) is separate from your body. And at that point redirecting the flow of energy by acupuncture can assist in wellness.

Auras

The last energy field I'm going to bring to your attention is your aura. This energy system is on the outside of our bodies. It's pretty cool and pretty versatile. We get a lot of use out of it, and there are different layers to our aura as well. It is amazing, but for now, we'll just stick with basics.

So one thing your aura does is act as your own personal force field. It expands and contracts depending on how we feel about ourselves, our surroundings, and other people.

Auras also can give a lot of information about a person. You know animals sniff one another for information. Well, with humans, we use the aura to feel one another for information.

Today, many people can see auras, and if you can't, you could train yourself to. I personally cannot see auras, but I can definitely feel them.

For instance, I was once doing a healing on a woman who was going through a tough divorce. Her aura felt like taffy to me. I was clearing it but I really had to work it. It was literally thick and dense. The woman had unknowingly been collecting negative energy from her difficult divorce, and she was holding all that negativity within her aura.

Did you ever meet someone you instantly didn't like? You feel yourself pulling away from them? At that moment you may not know why, but in reality you're reading their energy. First impressions are reading energy.

So how do we pick that up? Individuals broadcast or send out energy by their thoughts and actions, and you receive that information.

It's like breathing, it's happening and most of the time you don't even realize it.

Here's an example. Have you ever talked with someone and found when you started the conversation you were feeling okay but by the end you were aggravated? And you couldn't get away fast enough? Right?

You were reading their energy. In this case it wasn't very pleasant. In some instances, you can even absorb their energy without realizing it. And if you do, you should clear it or you may be carrying it until you do.

There are many ways to clear energy, but here's a quick and effective way to clear energy anytime or anywhere.

You begin by closing your eyes and visualizing any energy that doesn't belong to you anywhere on your body making its way to your arms, down your arms, and leaving your body out through your fingertips and returning back to the sender. Now with this you don't need to know who the sender is because in the course of the day it could be more than one person. And don't worry about the energy getting back to the right person because energy is like a stray dog, it will find its way home.

Looks Are Deceiving

Now let's explore our psychic senses. They're just the same as our physical senses with one exception. The psychic senses perceive things beyond the physical.

We use them all although some are more heightened than others just like your physical senses. The sense of feeling is probably the easiest psychic sense for people to get because you do that without really trying.

So regardless of how someone looks, psychic feeling is not superficial.

Let me clarify. Sometimes angry people don't look angry.

Were you ever really mad and then had to do a quick switcheroo so someone wouldn't see your anger?

Underneath, your feeling hasn't changed regardless of how good of a front you put on. That anger is still emitting outward. Anyone can pick up on it with their psychic sense.

Have you ever walked into a room and felt the tension? It's so thick you could cut it with a knife. There's no little guy in the room named Tension. You're feeling with your psychic sense the energy emitted by whoever is in the room or had been in the room.

If the room is empty, then you're picking up on an energy signature left behind. Energy residue can linger for years and if you're sensitive enough, you'll read it.

But whether you realize it or not, you're getting information all the time.

Sometimes you just know things. You don't know how you know, but you just do. The one thing that decides whether or not you acknowledge the information is your filters. And when I speak of filters, I mean, what do you believe?

Let's look at the case of Molly. Molly worked in Boston. She drove in and parked her car in a lot near work. One day in winter after Molly got out of work she was walking down the same street she always did but on this day she had a feeling that she should cross the street. She couldn't seem to shake the feeling. The only thing in her view were these two young men walking toward her. They were clean cut, they were preppy dressed, and they looked okay so Molly couldn't understand why this feeling wouldn't leave.

When these young guys got up to her they pushed her into a snowbank. She didn't know what they were intending to do so she began screaming and lashing out with her hands and feet not realizing what they were after was her pocketbook, which was slung across her shoulder. While she was trying to protect herself, one of the young men cut the strap of her pocketbook and they took off running.

Why didn't she listen? Because her logical mind took over. Her logical mind sized up the situation and based on all the data concluded what she saw was no immediate threat. Her logical mind took into account what was perceived but not necessarily true. So it went something like this.

She felt the feeling and then she scanned to see what the perceived threat was. All she saw were two young guys, groomed and well dressed. They looked like college kids to her, and in her mind she didn't see that as a threat. It was visual deception and it happens all the time.

However, on the psychic scale she felt that she should cross the street. She was picking up on their vibration, and it was translating as a warning. In other words, her psychic abilities were in full-blown mode.

Lots of people have a name for their intuition. Whether you call it your intuition, gut feeling, or inner voice, it's all the same. My husband happens to calls his intuition, his little voice.

So on this day my husband was going to play racquetball. His little voice started sending him a warning about one of the two guys he was going to play against. Before getting on the court my husband's little voice kept telling him "Tom's dangerous." "Tom's dangerous." He didn't actually hear anything, but that was the feeling he was getting. My husband, who's considered an "A" player, which is a really experienced player, felt there wouldn't be a problem because of his experience.

After playing he came home and asked me to take a look in his mouth because Tom had hit him during the game. Oh boy! Tom, the guy my husband was warned about, ended up hitting him in the mouth with his racquet and popped four of his front teeth not out of his mouth, just out of the sockets!

It took eleven shots of Novocain to pop his teeth back in (you can feel this, right?), and he had to have his top teeth wired for eight weeks. It was a tough lesson, but it taught him that when his little voice speaks, he's to listen, no questions asked.

So again, why didn't he listen? His logical mind kicked in, no pun intended, and weighed the information and decided even though he got the warning he still felt Tom really wasn't a threat.

Now I don't want you to think by these examples that you only get information when something bad is going to happen. That's not true. You get information that's helpful too.

I had to go to the social security office. It wasn't a matter that I had to get it done right now so I put it off for about six months because a few years prior when I had been to that office I had to wait for hours. The line had been outside, and it took me an hour and a half just to get into the building. So this time I called to see if I could get an appointment. They told me no, they didn't take appointments. After that I was really dreading going. It's winter, it's cold, and I don't want to stand in a cold line.

Then I got this feeling that I should go on this particular day. I thought about it but didn't commit myself at first *until* I kept getting the feeling.

Long story short, I went and was in and out in under an hour. Totally psyched!

We all get psychic information but then we have what is called free will, which means we get to **choose** whether we believe or not what we're getting. We also get to **choose** whether we want to accept or not what we're getting and finally we get to **choose** whether we'll act on what we're getting.

Sometimes when you get information you don't have anything to back it up, meaning that if you go with it you may not get a validation that tells you it was the right thing to do.

The gut feeling is a prime example. You get the gut feeling, but you can't logically back it up. You feel it but then the inner struggle begins. I know but ...

That's the famous "I know but ..." So you go with the "but" and find it was the wrong choice. Next thing you know you are berating yourself. "I knew it. I don't know why I didn't do it, I knew it." Sound familiar?

Don't beat yourself up too much because there's a lesson there. And the hope is, if you get that feeling, the next time you'll know to go with it.

You see, with psychic information there's a faith element. At that point, do you go on blind faith? How much trust do you have in it?

I Want to Be More Psychic

Because it isn't about becoming more psychic, because you already are, it's about you becoming more aware. More aware. More trusting. Going on blind faith. Accepting the "just knowing."

How do you accomplish this?

Well, first, you have to be open, willing, and ready to accept. But beyond that you may have to work at it.

To illustrate this point let's imagine we're on a psychic baseball team. I just happen to be the Babe Ruth on the psychic team because I'm the natural. It happens. You'll always find those who have the natural attitude, but it doesn't mean you can't achieve the same. Listen, you made it on the psychic team because, well, you're psychic. It doesn't mean I'm better at it, but it may mean you have to work a little harder to get to the same level. You see, I've been working my whole lifetime on it in one form or another. So the bottom line is, like everything else, you get out of it what you're willing to put in. You may have to relearn what you haven't been using.

Of course you do have some who want to be "psychic" because they think it's neat or it will get some cool attention, but you have to understand it's not a magic trick. Like everything else you learn, you need to understand it.

So let's move on to some important areas that affect psychic ability.

Control

The first is control. There are a couple of points on this I want to address. You can control certain situations; for example, if you're in a haunted house or plagued by ghosts.

So let me clarify.

In general, people get upset with the idea of ghosts or a presence in their house or at their workplace. They often feel that their space has been totally violated. I get calls about this all the time. People calling in a panic; they're scared by what they have seen, heard, or felt. They have unwelcome guests, and there's nothing they can do about it. Or is there?

At times I don't even have to go to the house to tell them why it's happening. A few questions over the phone can sometimes offer a solution.

Over the past twenty-five years I have concluded that there are certain aspects that can bring out spirit. Discord is number one. All that negative energy swirling around can get upsetting and not just to members in the house that you can see.

Another reason, believe it or not, is redecorating and remodeling. That's total grounds for stirring up spirit. You're changing their house, and they may not like it.

There are also stories to tell, relatives to deal with, and people who stir up things.

In any event regardless of what it is, I recommend first telling whoever is there that they are scaring you and to please stop. Usually, in the case of a relative, once Uncle Bob is identified the family members are generally okay with it—unless they really didn't like Uncle Bob!

If you're remodeling, letting them know you're just beautifying the place can sometimes simmer them down.

In the case of Isabel, who is extremely sensitive to spirit, she recently told me when she moved into her new place she instantly felt spirit there. She didn't know who it was, but she certainly didn't want to encounter anyone, especially because she has a toddler. Isabel did what I suggested and spoke to spirit letting them know that she would prefer they not show themselves in any way because she didn't want to be frightened. Later, she told me after letting them know, she never felt them again.

When it comes to psychic information you can always tune in and turn off if you choose.

Differences

Jumping now into another area that affects psychic ability is understanding that no two psychics are alike. What works for one doesn't necessarily mean it works for another. We all learn the basics but then it's like art, you have to make it your own.

To give you an example, let's use a symbol. When I'm reading for someone and I see a flamingo it's my symbol for Florida. For you, an orange may be your symbol for Florida, and for someone else, their symbol for Florida may be a map of the state. They all mean the same thing, but the symbol for each person is different.

Your psychic abilities will get individualized. You'll make associations that will be end up being **your** meanings, just as someone else will do. There is no right or wrong way. So don't think just because you may read energy in a different manner from another psychic, or because you use your psychic senses differently, that you're doing it wrong. It's simply how you pick up or interpret what you're getting.

Chatter

Chatter is probably one of the biggest obstacles getting in your way when it comes to your psychic abilities. Your mind needs to be free so it can expand and examine all the energy you encounter. If you find you're always thinking, you can't get into that space that's open. All that chatter is occupying your mind and preoccupying your body. Inspiration can't get through, solutions are hard to find, and you certainly can't tap into anything because it just can't get through. And if it does? It's probably ignored because your mind is busy elsewhere.

It's like when you're working on a problem and you can't get the answer. You stop trying and go on to other things and voilà! It comes to you. Same principal.

We all have somewhere in the range of 50–70 thoughts per minute and that translates to 40,000–70,000 thoughts per day depending on your waking hours. That's a lot of thinking!

Thoughts like, *What am I going to make for dinner? How do I get this scratch off my shoe?* and *Do I need to pick up anything on my way home?*

It can get pretty busy in there. In order to tap in, you have to be what I love to tell people: mindless. Sounds like a good bumper sticker, doesn't it? Be mindless. And you don't have to be blonde to do it! I want to share this funny aspect with you. When I tell people that they have to be mindless, they automatically start thinking about that.

Emotion

But just because you stop the chatter doesn't necessarily mean you're tapped in and open. From a psychic standpoint, if you're emotionally unavailable, hope of tapping in becomes dim. And the stronger your emotional state, the less you can hope of tying in.

To understand what I'm talking about, imagine with me for a moment that I'm sad after watching the movie *Inside Out*. If I can even manage to get past thinking about how sad I am and why I'm so sad, it doesn't mean I won't be sad. Why? Because I still may feel sad. I'm not thinking, I'm just feeling. The only thing that happened is my focus. That focus just shifted from my mind to my body.

And with your psychic senses more often than not feelings will play a pivotal role in reading and interpreting energy. So if you're emotionally unavailable you may not be able to tune in. Remember, it's all about the vibration.

Did you ever feel someone watching you? That creepy feeling comes over you and you know, you don't know how you know, but you just know, that someone is watching you.

Truly think about it. In a matter of seconds, you feel and determine that someone is watching you. You look around. You don't see anyone, but you still have that unsettled feeling. How were you able to determine this? Through a vibration. They were focusing on you, directing their energy toward you, and your psychic antenna picked right up on it.

Now this is where this example gets interesting. I just demonstrated how on one hand directed energy can feel totally creepy. But on the other hand, that same watching can create excitement. Let me explain.

Now I'm going to teleport you to a bar where you meet some of your friends. While you're having a drink you can feel someone staring at you. We've all had that at some point, right? You look around and discover, ooh la la! A tall hunky guy or beautiful woman, whichever the case may be, is checking you out. Now you get a rush of excitement.

Same thing is happening, you felt that someone was watching you, but there is a slight difference. You can see the individual.

You put away your psychic antenna and let your mind get involved. It then processes whether or not there's a threat.

Just a note, if you can't see someone, it becomes more threatening, although truthfully that doesn't mean there's a threat.

So getting back to the person watching you that you couldn't see. Well, it turns out it was a nice little old lady watching you out the window to make sure you were okay. And the person in the bar, that's the real creep.

When you're feeling vibrations, sometimes the first emotion that crops up is fear, because at times your first impression is not really an impression, it's a response. In this case the response is to what you can't see.

Your psychic senses go beyond the visual. I'm not saying that you may never feel a true threat. But I want to point out that the first emotion that we normally experience when dealing with something beyond our understanding is usually fear, especially with preconceived notions surrounding the paranormal.

Let's Go Beyond

Now, we're going to explore a couple of concepts that can help heighten your abilities. Just be open to them because you may need to be mindless in order to understand them. Did you just start thinking?

Time

To begin with, we'll start with time. In the psychic world, time doesn't exist. We live day to day in the linear world. The linear world is the component of past, present, and future. In linear where we stand right now is in the present, not the past nor the future. But in the psychic world, where we stand right now, past, present, and future are all happening simultaneously.

It's a lot to think about, but let me give you a simple way to understand this concept. Let's imagine for a moment that we're in our psychic mode. Our psychic mode puts us standing on top of a very high mountain. At our viewpoint we can see everything for miles and miles. To our left is the past, in the center is the present, and to our right is the future.

When we're in linear time we can only see where we are. It happens to be the present because we're always in the present. We can't see the past because it's around the corner. And we can't see the future because it is around another corner. In linear time that's how it exists for us.

But because all of us are in expansion standing on top of this mountain we can see everything; there are no corners to our perspective.

Linear time has limitations.

Without the confines of time you can see, I don't want to say beyond the present moment, because you're really not, but if you think in linear terms you would perceive it to be.

There are stolen moments when you actually do expand beyond the boundaries of time. Have you ever been unconscious of time because you were engrossed in something or had such a wonderful time that you didn't realize the time that had just passed?

You went beyond where time didn't exist. In my workshop, The Healing Journey, when we get done I always ask the group how long they felt we journeyed. They'll tell me it felt like ten to twenty minutes, possibly thirty at the very most, when in fact it's been at the very least an hour up to two hours.

What a Feeling

But time isn't the only way to help heighten your abilities. Being able to see energy is a way to read it.

Lots of people can feel things but they can't see things. Although they know what they're feeling, not being able to psychically see images does tend to create doubt in their minds about their psychic abilities.

I believe if you can feel it, you can see it. It may not be a case of not being able to see, it may be a case of fear of what you might see.

But if you're willing and want to, you can slowly open that window.

You can actually feel something into an image. The way is very simple. When you start feeling something, you first have to get past your fear in order to go deeper into the feeling. When you achieve that and you get there, you become mindless and just observe. You watch and see what comes to you.

So follow along with me and imagine for a moment that we're in this big old spooky house.

You're following slowly behind me and then you begin to feel something. What? You think about it for, oh let's say, a second, and then you tug on my shirt getting closer to me and whisper in a panic, "I feel like there's someone here." So I stop and you just about run into me, and I ask in a quiet voice, "You do?" You nod your head. Then I ask, "Is it a man or a woman?" You whisper back, "I think it's an old lady."

"Why do you think it's an old lady?" I whisper back pushing you to feel that vibration.

"I don't know." So I ask you again but this time I add, "Feel why you think it's a woman."

"Because I think she's wearing a dress."

This is feeling the energy into an image. As your fear dissipates, you actually can begin to get a picture because you're now reading the energy. You most likely will not see an apparition, but you will begin to see in your mind's eye. That's really important for you to know. You're reading the feeling and translating it into a picture gram.

It may go like this: I feel it's an old woman, I feel she has light hair, I feel she's wearing a dress, I feel she has a mustache. Okay, the last, I admit, I just wanted to see if you were paying attention.

But again, first and foremost you have to get past your emotion, and in this case the emotion you needed to get past was fear.

Signs

In lieu of having to rely on your psychic abilities, because some of you won't, it doesn't mean you have to give up on the hope of connecting. Psychic signs can give us both direction and messages. I think they are possibly the most playful, nonthreatening way we can connect with our higher power.

Signs come from the universe. I use the term universe as a broad sweep, but it encompasses the big kahuna, angels, guides, and loved ones that have crossed over.

The number-one problem I see is that people don't feel they're special enough for the universe to give them signs in order to help them out. So they don't honestly look for them, never mind ask for them.

You might have a problem you need help with. The universe wants to help you out so they send you a sign.

Sometimes the signs are in direct relationship to what you're thinking; sometimes they're in direct relationship to what you're asking for;

and sometimes they're in direct relationship to what you need.

Some signs are pretty basic, quick, and you get them instantly.

For example, you're driving in your car and you're thinking about some problem and then you think, *God, I wonder if you're really listening to me?* Because after all at some point or another we're all testing God to see if he's listening. And then a car turns in and gets in front of you and you notice it's one of the Visiting Angels. Can't mistake that sign.

But some signs are really messages, and they can be a collection of signs to get the message.

In this case I'll use one of my own as an example because the one I'm going to give you was really cool and very cleverly orchestrated. It also spanned weeks before I fully got the message. How interesting is that?

It started like this. I was in the Home Depot getting some paint mixed. There were about a half dozen or so people getting paint. I chilled and waited my turn. One by one the people left until it was only me and even the second paint mixer left. I told the guy what I wanted, and as the paint was mixing we began to chit-chat to pass the time. No big deal, but then our conversation takes a turn. The guy continues talking but totally leaves the topic we were discussing. Now what he's saying isn't making any sense. In the same moment I realized that I could feel this strange shift in the energy swirling around me. I stared at the paint mixer intently and then it dawned on me. Someone was talking through him. At this point I became a bit apprehensive. I psychically let my feelings be known, and whoever it was didn't press to come any closer but still kept speaking. I felt at that point that they understood the boundaries I was giving them so I then listened intently.

He continued speaking for several minutes, and then all of a sudden there was the shift again, only this time whoever had been speaking through him, left. The paint mixer returned and picked up on the conversation where it left off, only that was about five minutes ago.

When he had finished mixing my paint, I couldn't get out of there fast enough. I darted out to my car so I could write everything down that he said before I forgot any details. I didn't know what this was, but it obviously was intended for me.

When I got home I started trying to decipher what it all meant. There was a city mentioned, a church, and other details that I had no idea of. Nothing was clicking. After about an hour I finally put the paper away with a shrug. Maybe at some point it would make sense to me.

A few weeks later out of the blue I got this urge to contact this priest I had been told about a year earlier. This priest conducted readings. My friend had given me his name and phone number only. When I got the urge to contact him I didn't immediately act on it. But I kept getting the feeling that I ought to connect with him, so after a few days I gave in and called the number. After a few rings the phone was answered by a woman stating the name of the church. When I heard it, I hung up the phone, stunned. That moment when she said the name of the church I realized it was the same name the paint mixer at Home Depot had given me.

Talk about Twilight Zone! It took me a few minutes to recover. Then I quickly looked for that piece of paper with the information I had written down. Finally locating the paper, I scanned it quickly. The name of the church I had written down was the same name as the one I had just called.

Intrigued, I looked up the church online and discovered the town where the church was located was almost the same name I had written down with the exception of a letter or two.

At that moment I realized I was being pointed to this priest. So after thinking it all through, I called back and requested an appointment with him. The secretary told me that he was going on vacation and she would get back to me after she spoke with him. She really sounded doubtful that I would get an appointment before he left.

After I hung up the phone with her I decided to look in my planner to see what I had available before he left. All I had was a Tuesday at 3:00. Well, I now wasn't expecting anything on the return call.

About twenty minutes later his secretary called me back and said he could see me on Tuesday at 3:00. I think my mouth dropped open!

So the day comes and off I go off to see the priest. I don't know what to expect. I don't know why I'm being guided to him. But I have to see him to find out.

When I met him I liked him instantly. He has great energy. He took me in his office where we chatted for a few minutes and then he asked me why I was there. I told him what I did for a living so he would understand when I told him he had a message for me.

He was a little surprised by that because he wasn't picking up on anything prior to our appointment. So we chatted for a few more minutes before he started the reading. It went great, and then just before the end of the reading he told me he heard someone. "Wait a minute." He told me as he listened intently. Then he repeated verbatim what he had heard.

To my surprise it was a line from my father. The whole reading was a message from him. However, what truly fascinated me was how my dad had managed to get me to this man to deliver his words, how it all morphed. You see, my dad had been a teacher to me in this life, and even now that he has crossed over he's still teaching. Yes, this was a lesson for me. It was to demonstrate different ways spirit and others can give you messages. And I'm also sure that at some point he knew I would be sharing all this with you. So how much more extraordinary can it get?

Summary

So let's sum it all up.

Does this mean we go through our day getting psychic information? Yes and no. You're psychic, that's a given. Do you pay attention all the time? That's not a given.

We do have our filtering process. Where is our attention at the moment? What are we noticing? What are we drawn to? What do we feel? What's important to us? These are some of our filters, and we may or may not pay attention to any one of them.

Keep in mind, everything is energy and everything is vibration. People are energy, living things are energy, and even objects have energy or the very least, reside energy.

Now that you have the fundamentals behind your abilities, the real question is, do you believe? Do you believe what you're tapping into? Are you open to it? Are you accepting of it? Are you going to listen to it?

No one can answer those questions except you. But if you want to expand and experience more of your world in a whole new light then just be your psychic you.

SOUL

What Is Your Soul?

Your soul is your unique individual energy. It's timeless, it's boundless and most of all, it's who you really are. What makes your soul so interesting is that it's a storehouse of all your past experiences, all blended, all together, whether in this lifetime or other lifetimes that you've had throughout time. All that collective energy all put together is your soul.

Your soul isn't like your physical being. Your soul doesn't have hang-ups, fears, doubts, or negative aspects. It's not jaded by life or people or situations. In fact, its pure form is love. Your soul is the best part of you, the part that you always want to be, whole and happy.

Your soul is also connected to your higher power. However you address your higher power, whether it's God, spirit, creator, almighty, lord, or magnificent person of the universe, your soul connects to this higher power.

History

So how old is your soul? That all depends on how many lifetimes you've experienced. A young soul could only have a few physical lifetimes while an old soul like me has cycled through lifetime after lifetime. In fact, I was once told I was 10,000 years old. I think I look pretty good for my age.

Housing

So where is your soul? Your soul is housed in your physical body and is seated in your chest, just slightly to the left. When we (our soul or our energy) comes into our physical body we infuse all our cells with our life force.

Role Play

When we come here, meaning into the physical, it's like we're signing up to be in a play, only in this one, everyone gets a role. When we decide to come back, we'll join with our soul family, which could consist of up to a hundred people or more.

Our soul family is a group that we've been with before. For example, in another life my mother and I were sisters and then in this life, mother and daughter. You'll be with the same group only in different roles and even different gender until your lessons are complete. We chose our family, friends, and even the situations that we want to experience during our lifetime. All this in an effort to grow your soul.

And truthfully this could take many lifetimes. And when you're done learning from your group then you may move on to another to learn more lessons.

According to Worldometers, on January 9, 2016, the current population was over 7 billion people. And each of those individuals is engaging in his or her own play. Think about it, it's remarkable. All 7 billion people, having their own individual experience, as well as a group experience. And the amazing part, we're like dominos, we touch one another and create a chain reaction.

To give you an extreme example of how we affect one another I'm going to use the case of a murderer. That one person committing that one act changed how many lives? And how many of those lives that were altered then changed other lives as a result? There's the domino effect.

Soul Workings

But while we're all connected when it comes to our soul we're really like two people: our physical self that we see standing in the mirror in front of us, and our soul, the you that is standing in front of the mirror that you can't see.

So why would we have two different parts of us? Because our authentic selves are just pure energy so we need this body in order to be here in this physical plane and experience our lives.

When I'm reading for someone who has crossed over, I find names are not the number-one thing I'll get. Why? How many different names has that soul had? Which one do they like? Most times they prefer to identify themselves by their essence because their essence is like a fingerprint, no two are alike. And let's face it, you would know their energy anywhere. It has been imprinted on our soul.

To reiterate, your soul is the very best of you. At its core, it's the you before any life experiences. Outwardly, it's a combination of individual and collective energy. Meaning, you retain your individuality but you are also connected to all life forms and source. Your soul also retains impressions from every lifetime you have ever lived.

That means that if in another lifetime you had unresolved issues they may carry forward into your current life. Just as if you have current issues you fail to resolve in this lifetime they may carry to your next. Now that doesn't mean only problems; it could just be experiences or other aspects of your being that you had in another life.

Let me explain with my own experience.

For years I've always hated anyone putting their hands around my neck; even if they were only fooling around, it would really freak me out. It was so intense for me I wouldn't wear anything tight around my neck because it was too uncomfortable. I tried for many years and couldn't get past it so I just assumed that in another lifetime I must have been strangled. After all, doesn't everybody just assume that?

I also disliked the singing bowls. I don't know why, I just never really could embrace them.

So then I had been invited to this group of practitioners that met monthly. They would have either a group member or guest conduct some sort of demonstration. I never paid any attention to who or what was going on at any given

meeting, but on this particular day unbeknown
to me they were having a woman demonstrate
the gong, as well as the singing bowls.

When they announced it at the beginning of
the meeting my first reaction was to get up and
leave. No way did I want to sit through the singing bowls. What stopped me was this woman
I was sitting next to. We know each other, and
when I had arrived she was sitting somewhere
else and she moved so we could sit together. I
felt it would be rude to leave her after she made
an effort to sit with me.

I thought to myself, how bad could it be? So
first, the woman started playing the gong. Truthfully, I had never known that anyone could actually play the gong. But I was surprised; it was
really amazing and sounded really cool. So I was
happy. Then she went on to the bowls. While she
was playing I closed my eyes and I started drift-
ing ... and I found myself back in another lifetime.

I couldn't see myself because I was seeing out
the eyes of myself but I know I was a man. I was
in a courtyard of a monastery. It was shadowed,
it was quiet, and I could clearly see the old gray
stone surrounding me as well as under my feet.
I felt there was a fountain there somewhere because I could smell water. It seemed to me like
it was a space for contemplation. I don't know

why I was there, perhaps I was a monk. But in the distance I could hear the singing bowls.

I know I was standing with my hands to my sides, and suddenly without warning from behind I felt the penetration of a knife in my jugular vein. It penetrated deeply, and from the shock I fell to my knees, slowly sinking to the floor.

I never saw or heard my assailant coming or leaving. When I fell to the stone floor, I lay there. I lay there and could hear in the distance the sound of the singing bowls. With every heartbeat and every breath, a little more of my life force ebbed away. I lay there and listened as the music grew fainter and fainter until I couldn't hear it any more.

And then I'm back here. I realized several amazing things. First, my friend who had moved to sit with me was supposed to so I would stay and have my experience. Also it cleared up the mystery of why I never wanted anything near my neck, and last, the singing bowls. This is really cool. I heard them but they were my anchor in that distance place. And jumping back to the time doesn't exist, I already knew prior on some level the bowls were the anchor bringing me through time and space.

See that? My dislike of the singing bowls was really because I knew I would hear them when

I was brought back to that time because they were really my anchor to come back.

Truthfully, experiencing that event gave me an insight into that lifetime regardless how brief it was. Why it happened and exactly for what reason I haven't figured out yet, but there is something behind it. I don't believe in randomness. I just haven't figured it out yet.

On another note, the energy of that event imprinted itself on my soul. In this case minutes before I left my body so there was no time for me to absorb really what was happening, it was too quick. Therefore, when my soul entered this body, the energy from that event got infused and reactivated into all the cells of my new body.

Why? Because it was a negative event, and on this plane of existence there's a vibration that will match it and bring it forward.

Here on this plane of existence we have negative and positive energy, vibrations that we either embrace or repel. It's a dance. We constantly go back and forth throughout our day from one to the other. But the question is, which will prevail? The ultimate goal is to be positive **all** the time, but for most of us that's a quest. Just being positive may be one of our lessons. With that said, let's consider our soul lessons.

Soul Lessons

Before we come to this physical plane, we choose the lessons we want to learn in this lifetime. Each one of us has free will, which means even though we have those lessons set up for ourselves we can always choose to bypass them.

Sometimes it's hard for us to understand some of the lessons we experience during our lifetime simply because some experiences we wouldn't wish on our enemy.

But you have the choice to create and craft your life. I know you may wonder, "What if there was no choice?" Even then, there are lessons and choices that follow even when you don't have a choice at that time. Big and little choices are made every day. Sometimes it seems like we make millions of choices a day. Then once in while you decide you're tired of making choices. So you make a decision. I'm not going to make any choices today. Actually you had to make a choice to decide not to make a choice. See how that works?

We also have karma to work through. Karma means that for every action there is a reaction.

You may have heard that sassy expression, "that's gonna come back to bite you right in the a.s.s." It's the same thing. Action/reaction.

You may not see when it comes back around, but that doesn't mean it won't. Often I've seen it with myself and others, although some don't seem to recognize it when it does come around.

To give you an example, years ago when I was nineteen or so a friend of mine was selling, I don't even remember what, something out of the trunk of his car. Back then when someone was selling something out of the trunk of their car there usually was a question of where or how they got it. The seller gave me this story that I wanted to believe because the price was so great. I didn't ask any questions. Deep down I knew it was, as we referred to stolen property, "hot," but I decided I wanted to believe what he had told me so I bought it anyway. Cash of course.

About a year later before heading out to work, I had a feeling that I should hide my jewelry. I lived in a secure apartment complex, but even so I followed my feelings and hid all my good pieces. When I got home I discovered my apartment had been broken into. My jewelry box had been totally emptied, and all my costume jewelry in it was gone! But not the pieces I had hidden. They remained where I had hidden them.

It seems someone had left the laundry room door open, and that door led to the parking lot where the intruder entered. About four of us had been the victims of the break-ins.

Just a coincidence? Not in my world. This was clear case of karma. For the action of purchasing a stolen item, I was to experience what it felt like to have my property stolen.

Your soul also stands as a sentry allowing you to live and experience all on your own in this life, but when you really get out of whack and you turn too much from your authentic self your soul may try to reel you in by sending you messages in the form of feelings.

You may feel a yearning.

You may feel dissatisfaction.

You may even feel unfulfilled.

By whatever means your soul is trying to communicate with you, you'll know it because you will feel out of accord on some level.

Think of it this way. When everything is going right, you feel very good, and when things are going wrong, you don't. When you don't feel in accord, you need to examine things at that point because it may be a message from your soul.

Listening to your soul can help keep you on your chosen path and help you live your life to its fullest.

Because your soul is perfect. You are perfect. And we all are perfect, just as we are.

References

www.merriam-webster.com
www.history.com
www.nostradamus.org
en.wikipedia.org
www.edgarcayce.org
www.cia.gov/library
www.acos.org
http://science.howstuffworks.com
www-nlb.loni.ucla.edu
www.worldometers.info

Author Bio

Diane Lewis is a gifted psychic medium, considered one of the best in her field. She discovered her abilities at a young age; as she matured, she sought to better understand these psychic experiences in order to further develop and refine her gifts. Today, with over twenty-five years of experience, Lewis's true talent lies in her ability to help people—connecting them with the spiritual realm and leading them to uncover their own inner greatness. She uses her gifts in private intuitive readings, medium readings, public presentations, and workshops. You can learn more about her spiritual work on her website: www.dianelewis.us.com.

Books by Diane Lewis

From Psychic to Soul
Published by:
Ozark Mountain Publishing

A Little Inspiration
Published by:
CreateSpace Independent
Publishing Platform

Other Books by Ozark Mountain Publishing, Inc.

Dolores Cannon
A Soul Remembers Hiroshima*Between Death and Life*
Conversations with Nostradamus, Volume I, II, III*The
Convoluted Universe -Book One, Two, Three, Four, Five*
The Custodians*Five Lives Remembered*Jesus and the
Essenes*Keepers of the Garden*Legacy from the Stars*The
Legend of Starcrash*The Search for Hidden Sacred
Knowledge*They Walked with Jesus*The Three Waves of
Volunteers and the New Earth
Kathryn/Patrick Andries
Naked in Public
Patrick Andries
Owners Manual for the Mind
Dan Bird
Waking Up in the Spiritual Age
Julia Cannon
Soul Speak – The Language of Your Body
Ronald Chapman
Seeing True
Carolyn Greer Daly
Opening to Fullness of Spirit
Diane Lewis
From Psychic to Soul
Donna Lynn
From Fear to Love
Maureen McGill
Baby It's You
Andy Myers
Not Your Average Angel Book
Guy Needler
Avoiding Karma*Beyond the Source – Book 1, Book 2*The
Anne Dialogues*The History of God*The Origin Speaks
James Nussbaumer
The Master of Everything*Mastering Your Own Spiritual
Freedom

Victoria Pendragon
Born Healers*Feng Shui from the Inside, Out*Sleep Magic
Michael Perlin
Fantastic Adventures in Metaphysics
Charmian Redwood
A New Earth Rising*Coming Home to Lemuria
David Rivinus
Always Dreaming
Garnet Schulhauser
Dance of Eternal Rapture*Dance of Heavenly Bliss*Dancing Forever with Spirit*Dancing on a Stamp
Annie Stillwater Gray
Education of a Guardian Angel*The Dawn Book*Work of a Guardian Angel
Natalie Sudman
Application of Impossible Things
L.R. Sumpter
We Are the Creators
Janie Wells
Embracing the Human Journey*Payment for Passage
Maria Wheatley
Druidic Soul Star Astrology
Sherry Wilde
The Forgotten Promise
Lyn Willmoth
A Small Book of Comfort
Stuart Wilson & Joanna Prentis
Atlantis and the New Consciousness*Beyond Limitations*
The Essenes -Children of the Light*The Magdalene Version*
Power of the Magdalene

For more information about any of the above titles,
soon to be released titles, or other items in our catalog,
write, phone or visit our website:
PO Box 754, Huntsville, AR 72740
479-738-2348/800-935-0045
www.ozarkmt.com